What Happens When Someone Dies?

A Child's Guide to Death and Funerals

Written by
Michaelene Mundy

Illustrated by
R. W. Alley

ABBEY PRESS

Publications
St. Meinrad, IN 47577

Dedicated to all the little people in my life,
past, present, and future.

Text © 2009 Michaelene Mundy
Illustrations © 2009 Saint Meinrad Archabbey
Published by Abbey Press Publications
1 Hill Drive
St. Meinrad, Indiana 47577

Library of Congress Catalog Number
2009908379

ISBN 978-0-87029-424-2

Printed in the United States of America.

A Message to Parents, Teachers, and Other Caring Adults

Can you recall the first time you attended a funeral? What memories are most vivid to you? What impressions do you remember? The same issues will undoubtedly be going through the minds of the children you are concerned about when they are confronted with death and funerals.

I remember being more upset seeing my mother crying than anything else. Children need to be reassured that, while people are sad that someone will no longer be there to hug and to hug us back, our own love and care for the child is still present. And the care and love for us from the departed person will always be part of our lives. As we deal with our grief, it is important to find time to reassure children that we can and will be happy again.

Children are great observers, and through observing, decide how they will react to new and mysterious things. And death and funerals contain lots of mystery. We can help kids recognize that it is okay to cry and be sad and also to laugh at memories and be glad to see people that they haven't seen for a long time. Our talking with children about our own feelings will encourage them to talk about their feelings and ask questions.

Kids hear more than we give them credit for. Often, though, they may misinterpret situations because of their limited experiences. By listening to a child, we might discover what they are reading into a new experience. A child may wonder why people use the word "celebrate" or "celebration" at a funeral when everyone is so sad. You can explain to them that celebration is usually associated with happy times, and at a funeral, we celebrate happy times from the past to help us get through the sad times of the present.

In helping the children in our lives deal with death and what follows, we often find that children help us deal with and get through a difficult time that we ourselves are facing. In teaching, we learn much. So cherish the opportunity and grow with your child.

—Michaelene Mundy

Why Do People Die?

All living things begin, grow, change—and then die. You can see it happen in grass and flowers and plants. Sometimes things live for a long time (like a tree) and sometimes for not a very long time (like a flower).

People can die because they are very sick, very old, or sometimes because of an accident. They die when an important part of their bodies no longer works right to keep them alive—like the lungs to breathe or the heart to pump blood.

Not even doctors understand everything about death. It is something that happens—and something we can help each other deal with.

Does It Hurt to Die?

For many people, the biggest "hurt" about dying is knowing they will miss loved ones. Some people are ready to leave this world—because their bodies are tired or worn out and they hurt a lot; others are not ready at all.

Even some people who know God loves them are afraid to die. We pray that those who have died will "rest in peace." Death is hard to understand, so we compare it to something we DO understand. It is sort of like sleeping—but that person doesn't ever wake up. When a person is dead, their body doesn't move anymore. They look quiet and peaceful.

What Can I Do about My Sad Feelings When Someone I Love Dies?

Drawing pictures of things you did together, talking to other people about the person who died, crying, remembering happy times with that person, saying a prayer asking God to help you AND the person who has died, pretending you are talking to the person who died . . . all of these things can help. What good things are you remembering?

Our faith tells us that a person's body may die, but that their spirit or soul goes to another place to be with God. The body is what we can see and touch. The spirit or soul is what makes them special.

Are There Other Ways People Say Goodbye?

After a death, people get together—at a funeral home, at church, and at the cemetery—to say goodbye to the person who has died. It may feel like a party because there will be a lot of people you don't see very often.

Some people have different, special ways to say goodbye to the person who has died. Some have what is called "cremation" of the body. This means the body is turned into ashes and put into a pretty container that is buried or kept in a special place. Or the person who died is dressed nicely and buried in a special box called a casket.

What Happens at the Funeral Home?

When it is "Visiting Time" at the funeral home, ask your parents what it will be like. If there is something you are worried about, ask a grown-up about it.

You will notice lots of flowers in the funeral home. People send flowers to say they are sorry everyone is feeling sad. There may be pictures of the person when he or she was alive, along with his or her family and friends.

And there will be people crying, too, because they are sad. It's OK to cry at this time—and it's OK if you don't cry, too.

What Should I Say or Do at the Funeral Home?

At the funeral home, people talk about what they remember about the person who died. They talk about nice and sometimes funny times they had with the person. You may hear laughter as they remember happy times.

If you walk up to the casket, take your mom or dad's hand. We all need each other—especially in sad times. Sometimes the casket is up too high for you to see. Ask someone to help you up.

Usually there is a short line of people related to the person who died. If you want to say something to them, you can just say, "I'm sorry," or, "I'm sad, too."

Why Are People Crying—When They Believe the Person Is in Heaven Now?

Everyone who loved this person is sad. Even though they believe the person who died is now happy and with God in heaven, they may still be sad.

The person who died will be missed. They can't hug or be hugged anymore. They can't say they love us. We talk to them, but we can't hear them talk back. And we are sad for the family and friends who no longer have this person with them.

Maybe you have had a pet that died, and you miss your pet very much. Things are very different without the pet you loved. It's a lot like that.

Why Are Some People at the Funeral Home Happy and Laughing?

Laughing and remembering help us "be OK" and start to feel better.

Although death is not "funny" at all, we can tell funny stories of happy times we had with the person who has died. It makes us feel better. And we know the person who died would want us to be happy anyway.

You might hear people say about the person who died, "He had a good, long life," or, "She was always laughing and having a good time, wasn't she?" These are things to be happy about, even though we are very sad because the person will be missed.

What Will It Be Like at the Church Funeral Service?

Faith, love from the people around us, and belief in God's love for us and the person who died can help us get through the sadness.

The funeral service at the church helps us say thanks to God for this person's life. And it helps us truly believe that God will take care of the person who has died—and all of us who are sad now.

At church, people pray together, sing together, remember together, tell God together that they loved this person and they love God, too. Listen carefully to the words of the songs and prayers.

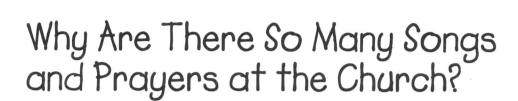

Why Are There So Many Songs and Prayers at the Church?

We sing and pray to thank God for giving us our lives—and the special life of the person who has died.

There are many beautiful ways to tell God that we are sad—but that we are happy, too. We come together to say we hope and believe the person who died is now in heaven.

Some of the songs and prayers will be words that God may be saying to the person who died or to the people who are missing someone. The songs may say not to be afraid and that God loves all of us.

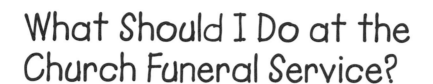

What Should I Do at the Church Funeral Service?

Listen and join in the prayers and songs. Listening to people read from the Bible helps us to realize that God loves us all very much and will always be there to help us.

Watch for different "symbols" that are used. You might smell smoky incense (special ashes) being used. You might see family members put a cover on the casket. You might see the priest or minister sprinkle water on the casket.

Listen carefully as a priest or minister or an uncle or aunt will say some kind words and maybe tell a story about the person who died.

What Happens at the Cemetery?

The cemetery is a quiet place where people are buried. The casket is put into a hole that is dug in part of the lawn. This is the grave. Loved ones gather around and say prayers, and say goodbye.

Often people walk by the casket one more time. Sometimes the casket is not put into the hole and covered with dirt until the family and friends are gone.

Later there will be a special stone at the grave. Many people continue to visit the cemetery for many years and say a little prayer and even leave flowers. It is a quiet place to remember the person who died.

What Will Heaven Be Like?

Most people believe our souls live on forever in heaven. What is a soul? It's the part of the person that makes them special and different from others.

Some people say God will give us "everything we really want" when we are in heaven. It may be that all of the special people in our lives will be together in one spot.

In short, heaven is a beautiful place where God takes wonderful, gentle care of people when they die. It is a place where everyone is happy.